CHRISTMAS DU...
for Violins
and other C instruments

by Will Schmid
Bowings by Darcy Drexler

Contents

HAL•LEONARD®
CORPORATION
7777 W. BLUEMOUND RD. P.O. BOX 13819 MILWAUKEE, WI 53213

About the Author

Will Schmid

Will Schmid is the author of the internationally acclaimed **Hal Leonard Guitar Method System** (available in 8 languages). He received his BA from Luther College and his PhD from the Eastman School of Music. Dr. Schmid has authored over 40 books, cassettes and a videotape for guitar, banjo, wind and string instruments. He has given workshops throughout the United States and in Canada, Australia and Europe. He is a Past President of the Wisconsin Music Educators Conference. He is currently Professor of Music at the University of Wisconsin-Milwaukee and serves on the editorial staff of the Hal Leonard Publishing Corporation.

Dedication

This collection of Christmas songs is dedicated to all of the wonderful string teachers who every year give children the opportunity to learn about this rich cultural heritage.

In particular I would like to thank those violin teachers who have worked with my three violin playing sons, Thacher, Kyle and Schuyler. Their patience, understanding and teaching expertise have given a great deal to our family.

They are Darcy Drexler and the *Young Violinists* program at the Wisconsin Conservatory, Glenn and Laurie Asch, Bonnie Greene, Bob Wernerehl at the *Stringalong Weekend*, Kathy Kalfas and Doris Nodalny at Elm Creative Arts School and Mike Betz and Laura Kautz-Sindberg at Roosevelt Middle School.

In addition, I would like to thank my UWM faculty colleague, Gerald Fischbach, for all he has done for string pedagogy worldwide.

How to Use This Book

This book is playable by 1 or 2 violins (or other C instruments such as flute or guitar) with chordal accompaniment provided by guitar, piano or other harmony instrument. This book is also available in viola and cello/bass editions which are compatible with this book. Therefore, this series can be used with young string orchestra classes. Each arrangement features the melody, a harmony (2nd) part and chords as follows:

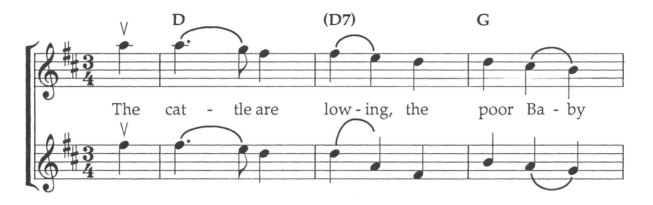

On page 31 is a guitar chord chart which may prove helpful to guitarists playing the accompaniment to these pieces.

Below is a chart which shows you some of the possible ways in which this book can be used.

1 violin	•Play the Melody. •Record one part and play the remaining part. This can be done with the simplest cassette recorder or in a more sophisticated way with the new multi-track recorders. You may wish to add the chordal accompaniment and bass or percussion if you have 4-track equipment.
2 violins	•Play the Melody and the Harmony parts; then repeat and switch parts. •Record the chordal accompaniment part and play the other two along with the recording. You may wish to add a bass part playing from the chord symbols.
Mixed strings	•Play both parts with accompaniment in mixed octaves.
Mixed instruments	•Mix strings, flutes, guitars, piano, recorders, oboes, trombones, bassoons or any other C instruments on these parts using the viola and cello/bass editions. Transposing instruments such as trumpets or clarinets can also be used if the parts are transposed.

Angels We Have Heard On High

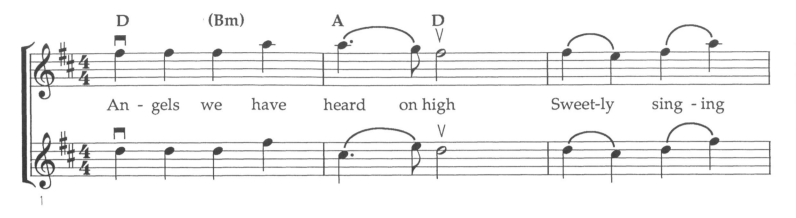

An - gels we have heard on high Sweet-ly sing - ing

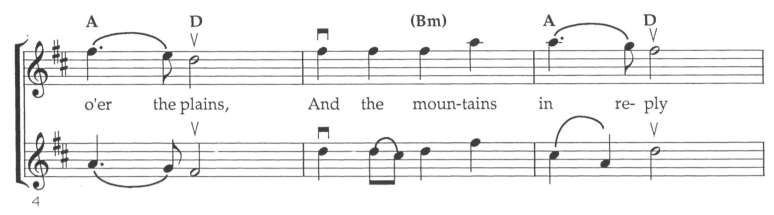

o'er the plains, And the moun-tains in re- ply

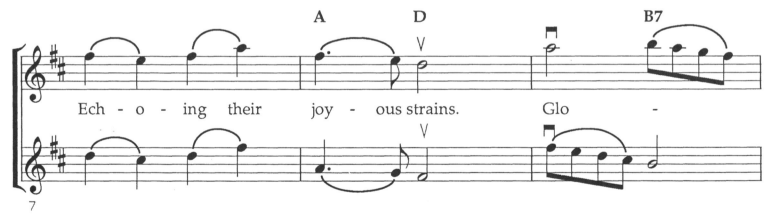

Ech - o - ing their joy - ous strains. Glo -

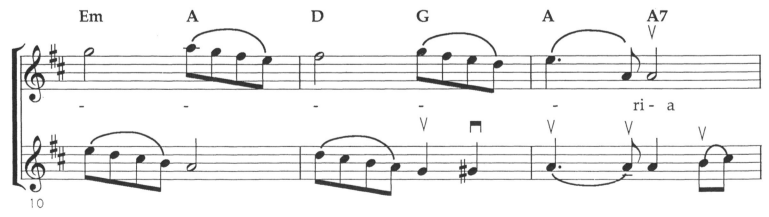

- - - - ri - a

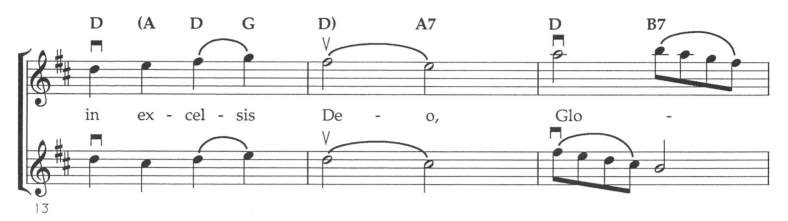

in ex - cel - sis De - o, Glo -

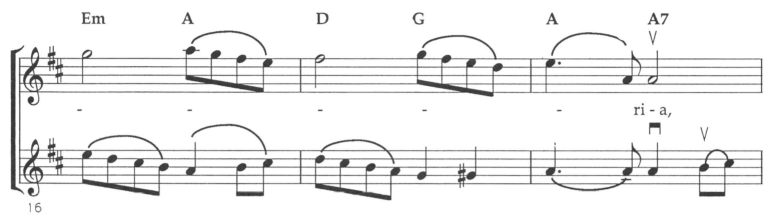

- - - - - ri - a,

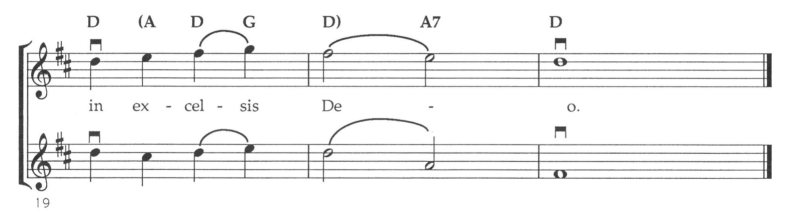

in ex - cel - sis De - o.

Away in a Manger (I)

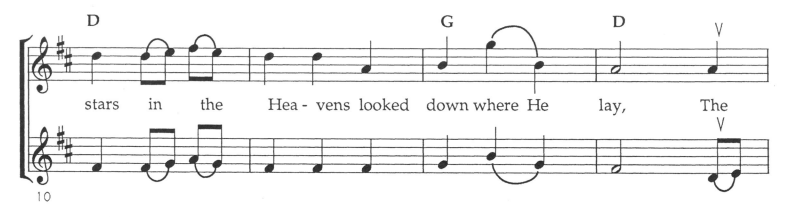

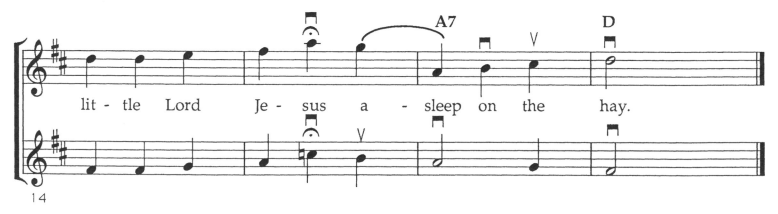

Away in a Manger (II)

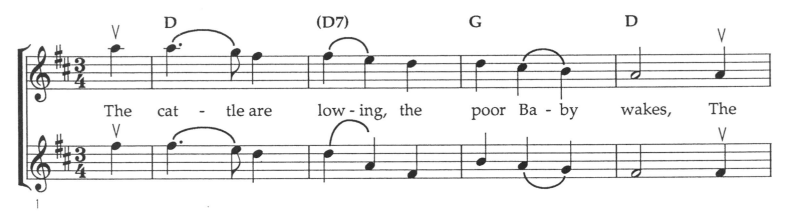

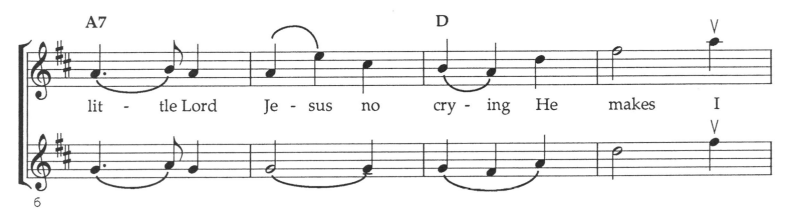

Bring a Torch Jeannette, Isabella

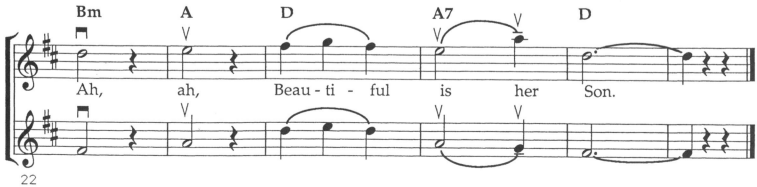

Deck the Hall

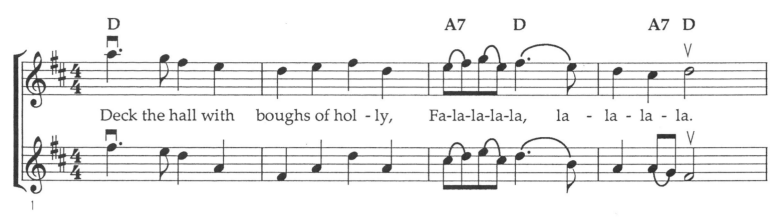

Deck the hall with boughs of hol - ly, Fa-la-la-la-la, la - la - la-la.

'Tis the sea -son to be jol - ly, Fa-la-la-la-la, la - la - la - la.

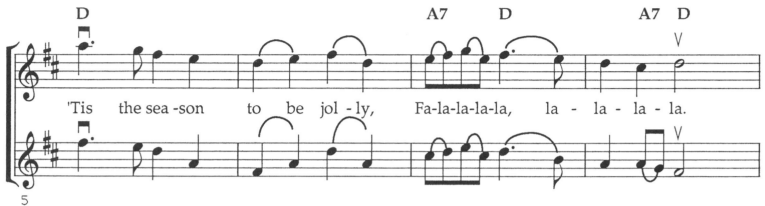

Don we now our gay ap-par - rel, Fa-la-la - la-la-la, la - la - la.

Troll the an - cient Yule-tide car - ol, Fa-la-la-la-la, la - la - la - la.

Go Tell It on the Mountain

Go, tell it on the moun - tain, Ov-er the hills and

ev - ery where, Go, tell it on the moun - tain, that

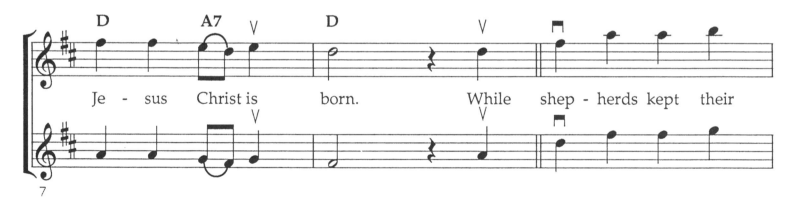

Je - sus Christ is born. While shep - herds kept their

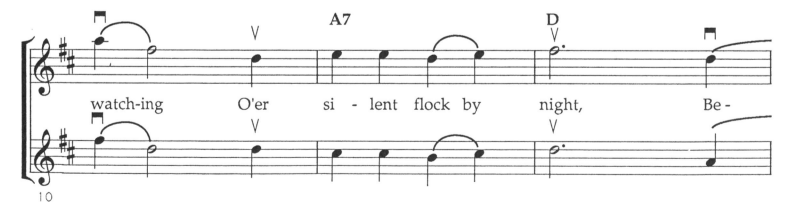

watch-ing O'er si - lent flock by night, Be -

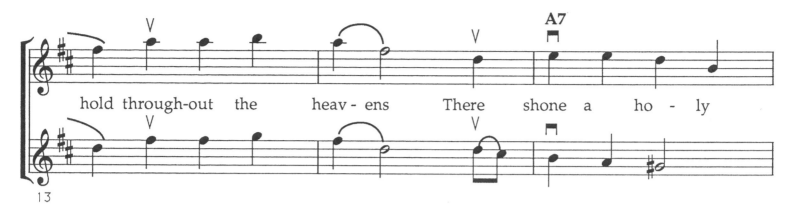

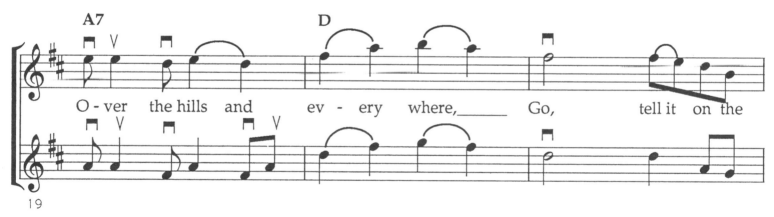

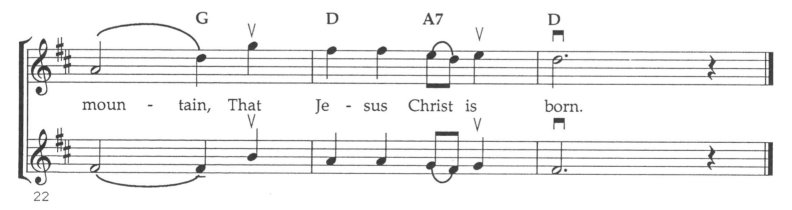

God Rest Ye Merry, Gentlemen

*Guitar–capo 2 and play chords in parentheses.

Good King Wenceslas

The Holly and the Ivy

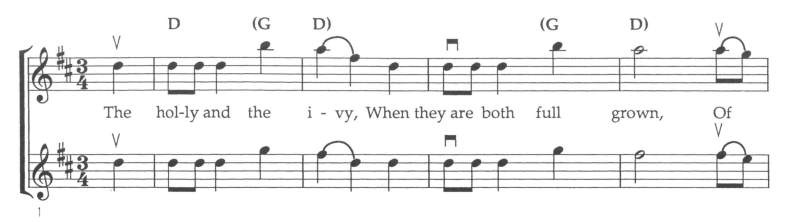

The hol-ly and the i - vy, When they are both full grown, Of

all the trees that are in the wood, The hol-ly bears the crown; The

ris-ing of the sun, And the run-ning of the deer; The

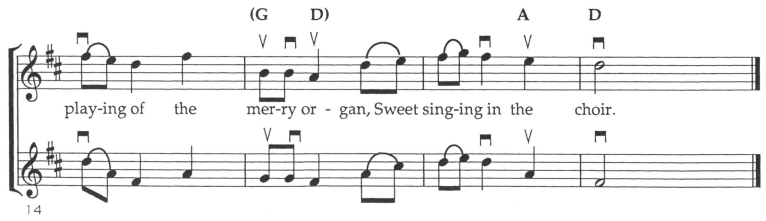

play-ing of the mer-ry or - gan, Sweet sing-ing in the choir.

Jolly Old Saint Nicholas

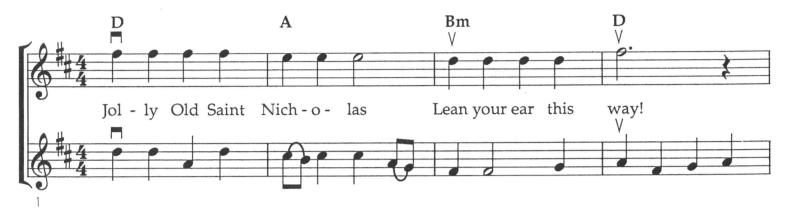

Jol - ly Old Saint Nich - o - las   Lean your ear this   way!

Don't you tell a   sin - gle soul   what I'm going to   say;

Christ-mas Eve is   com-ing soon,   Now, you dear old   man,

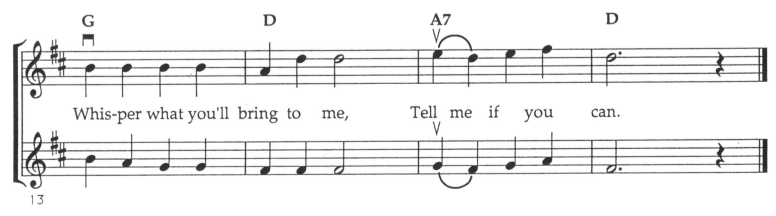

Whis-per what you'll bring to   me,   Tell me if   you   can.

Jingle Bells

Dash-ing through the snow in a one-horse o -pen sleigh.

O'er the fields we go Laugh-ing all the way.

Bells on bob - tail ring, mak-ing spir - its bright. What

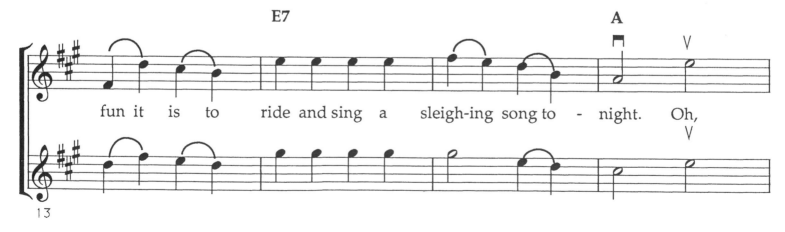

fun it is to ride and sing a sleigh-ing song to - night. Oh,

Joy to the World

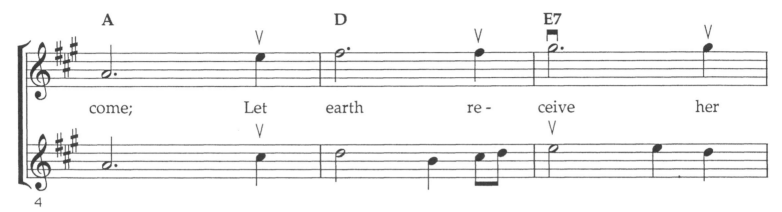

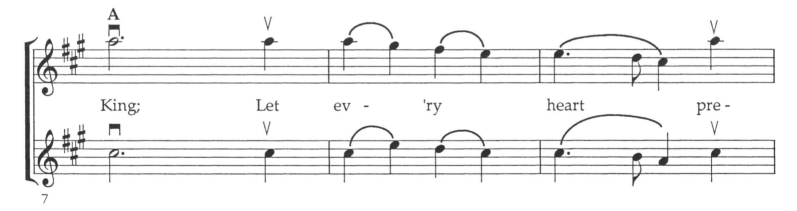

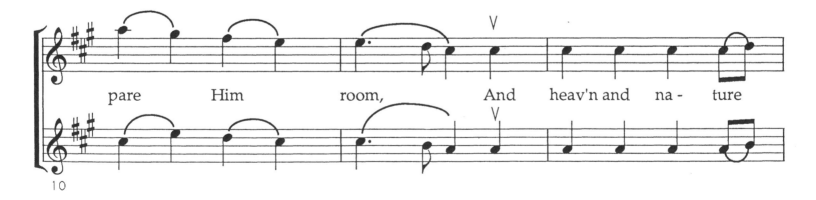

sing.   And   heav'n and   na –   ture   sing,   And

13

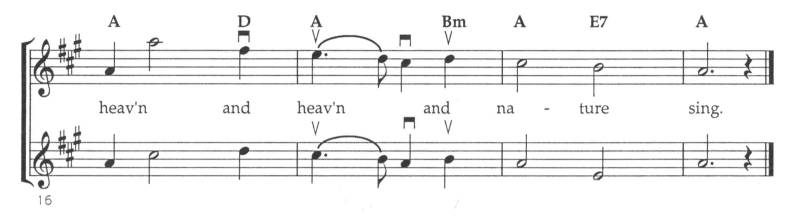

heav'n   and   heav'n   and   na –   ture   sing.

16

O Come, Little Children

O come, lit - tle chil - dren, O come, one and all, To

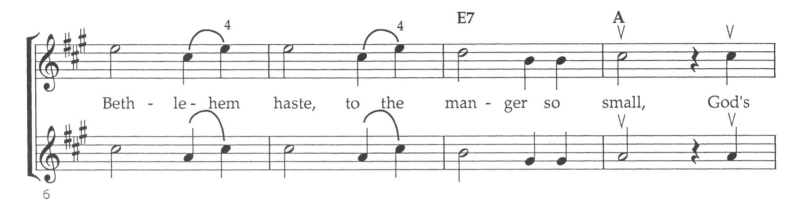

Beth - le - hem haste, to the man - ger so small, God's

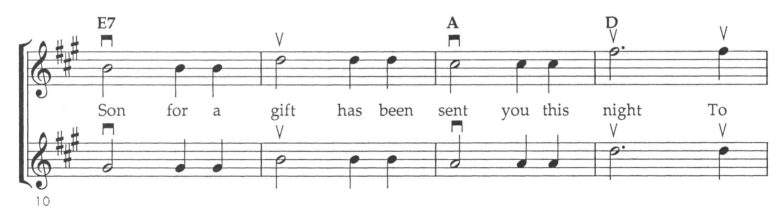

Son for a gift has been sent you this night To

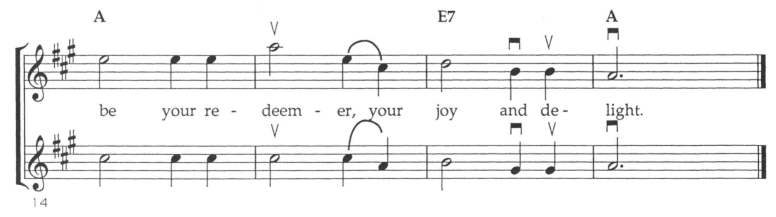

be your re - deem - er, your joy and de - light.

Patapan

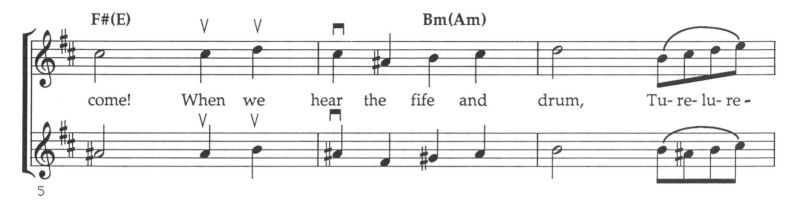

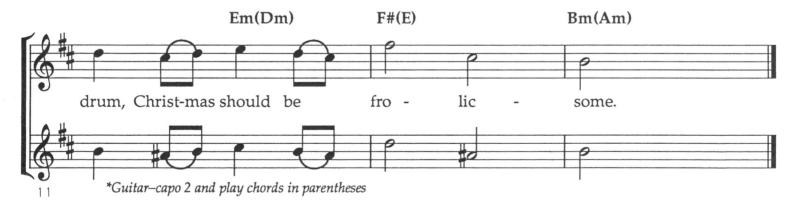

*Guitar–capo 2 and play chords in parentheses

Silent Night

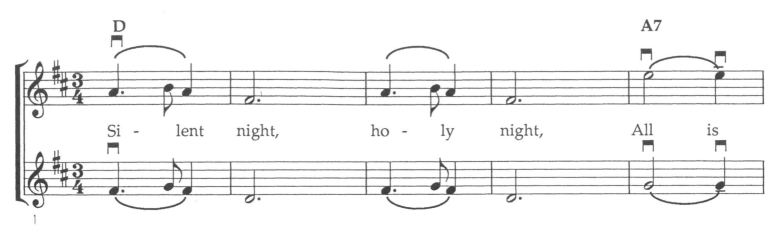

Si - lent night, ho - ly night, All is

calm, all is bright. Round yon vir - gin,
Ho - ly in - fant so

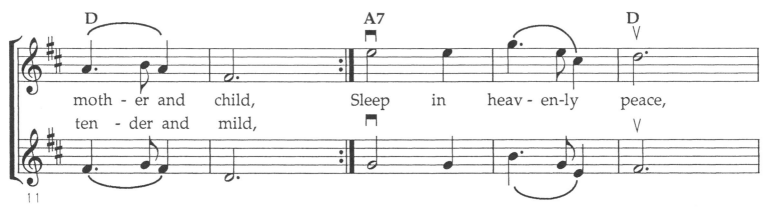

moth - er and child, Sleep in heav - en - ly peace,
ten - der and mild,

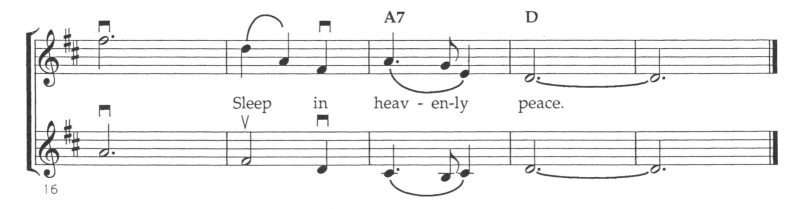

Sleep in heav - en - ly peace.

We Wish You a Merry Christmas

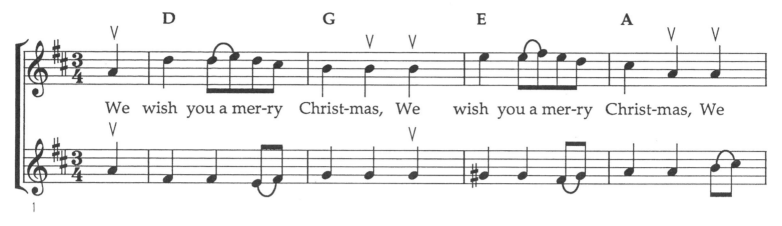

We wish you a mer-ry Christ-mas, We wish you a mer-ry Christ-mas, We

wish you a mer-ry Christ-mas and a Hap - py New Year.

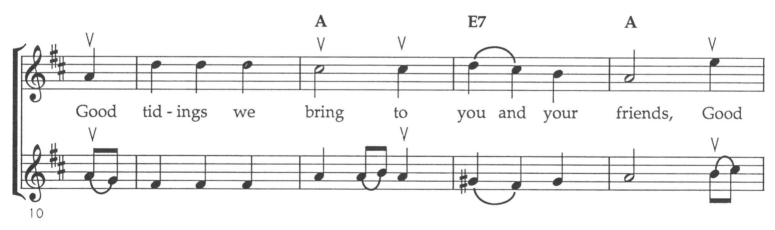

Good tid - ings we bring to you and your friends, Good

tid - ings for Christ-mas and a Hap - py New Year.

What Child is This?

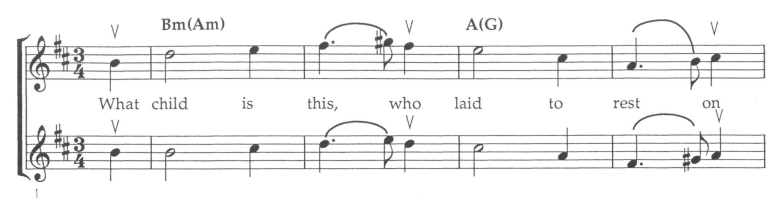

What child is this, who laid to rest on

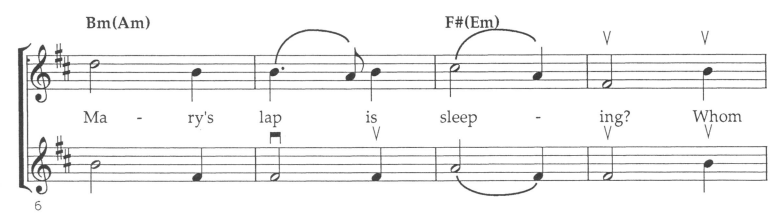

Ma - ry's lap is sleep - ing? Whom

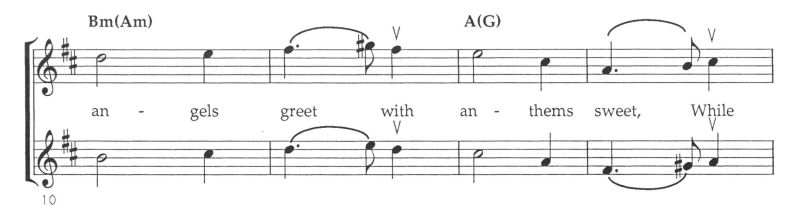

an - gels greet with an - thems sweet, While

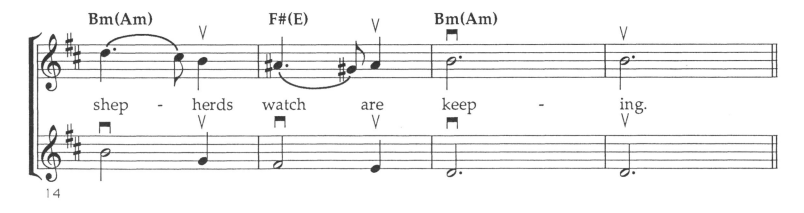

shep - herds watch are keep - ing.

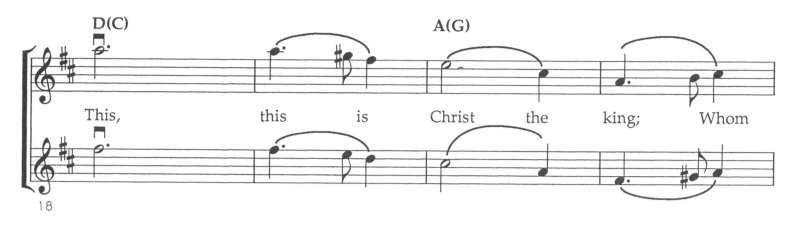

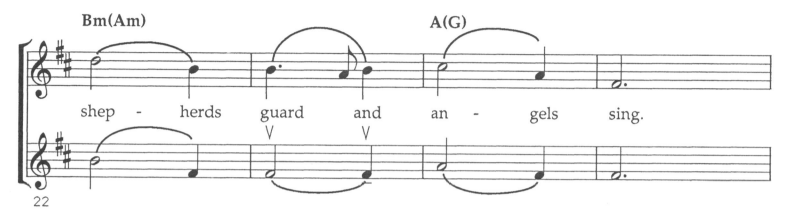

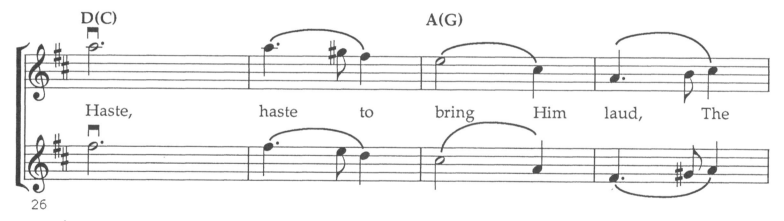

The Friendly Beasts

This arrangement of **The Friendly Beasts** features a different variation for each of the five verses of the song. It can be played by two players or more following these guidelines:

- **Verse 1** – Play the melody in *unison* (with chordal accompaniment if you have it).

- **Verse 2** – Play the *duet* in the usual fashion. The top staff is the melody and the bottom staff is a countermelody.

- **Verse 3** – Play the 2nd and 3rd lines of music as a *duet*. The top staff is an optional *trio* part which can be used if you have a third player available. The melody is passed back and forth between the 2nd and 3rd staves. Notice that this variation uses a different parallel type of harmony.

- **Verse 4** – Play as a *round*. With two players, the second player starts when the first reaches the asterisk in measure 5. If more that two players are available, the third and fourth players enter in the same fashion as the previous player reaches the asterisk.

- **Verse 5** – Play in *unison* as in verse 1.

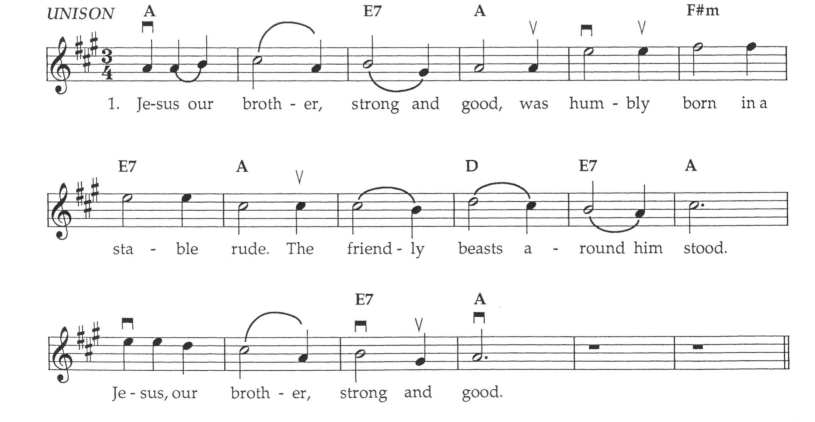

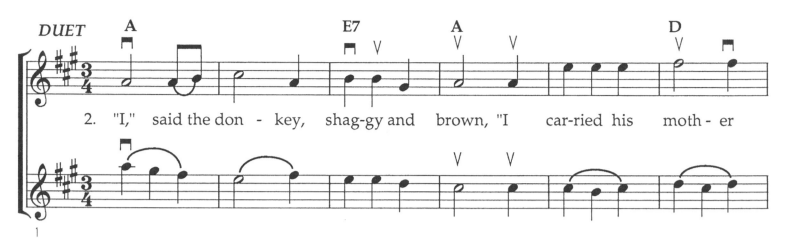

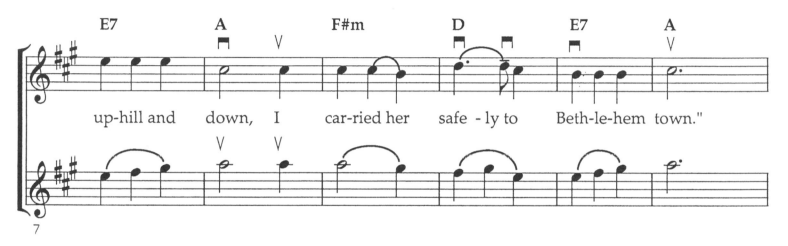

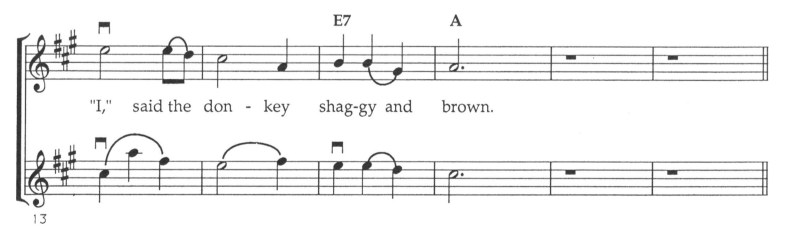

27

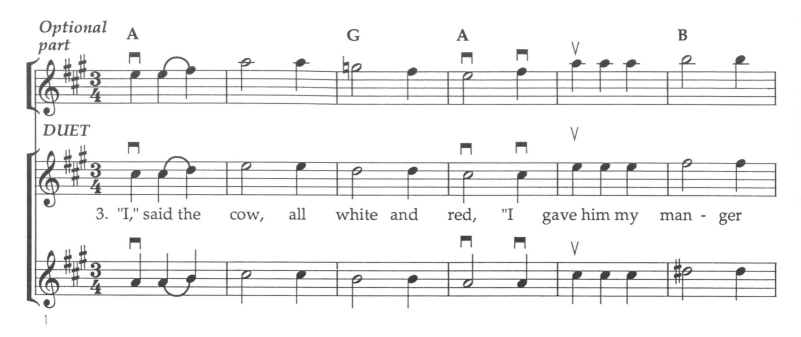

Optional part

DUET

3. "I," said the cow, all white and red, "I gave him my man - ger

for his bed, I gave him my hay to pil-low his head."

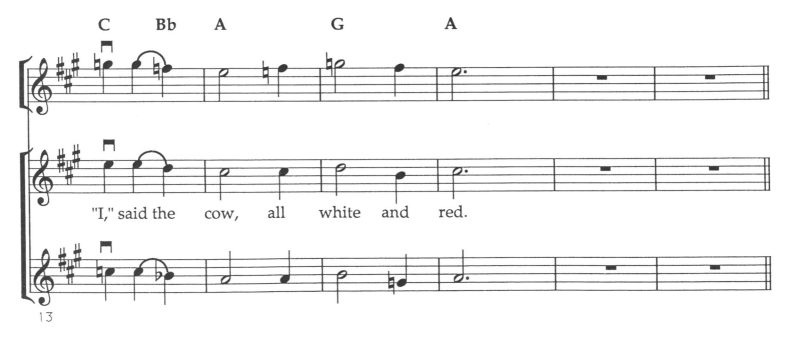

"I," said the cow, all white and red.

ROUND

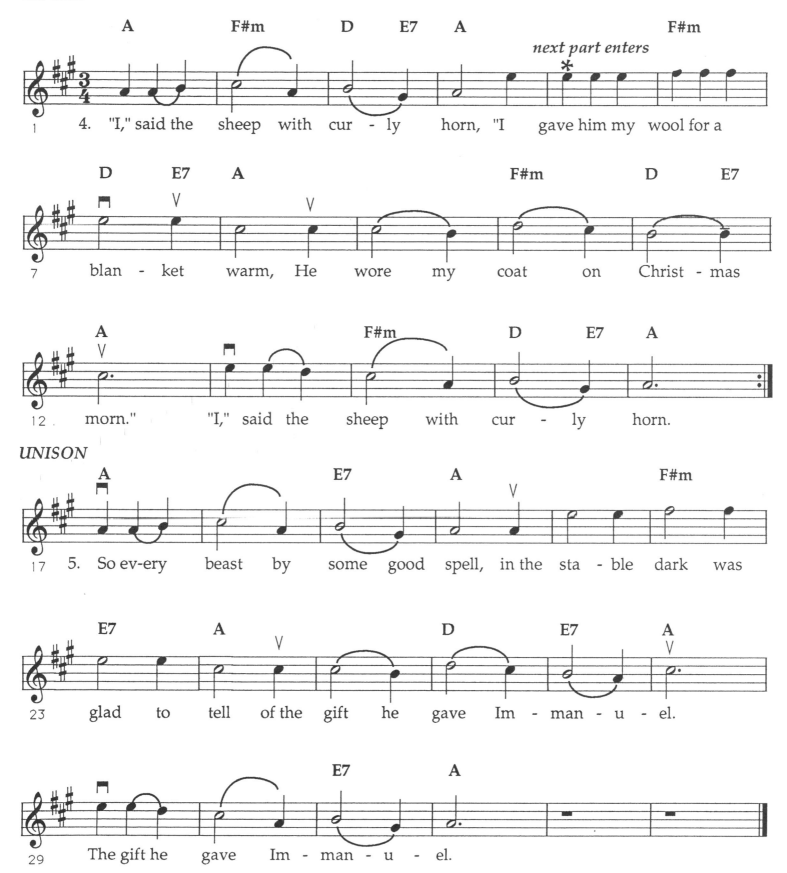

4. "I," said the sheep with cur-ly horn, "I gave him my wool for a blan-ket warm, He wore my coat on Christ-mas morn." "I," said the sheep with cur-ly horn.

UNISON

5. So ev-ery beast by some good spell, in the sta-ble dark was glad to tell of the gift he gave Im-man-u-el. The gift he gave Im-man-u-el.

Still, Still, Still

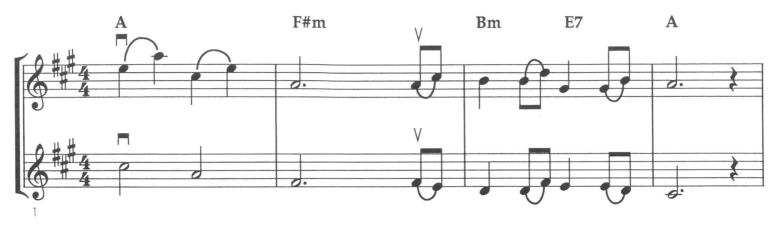

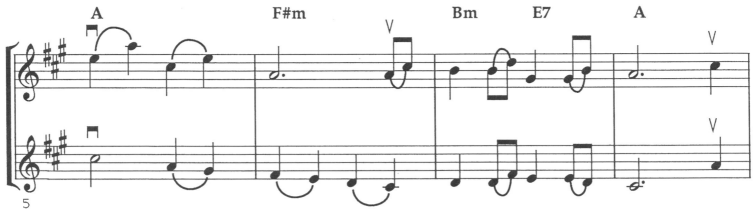

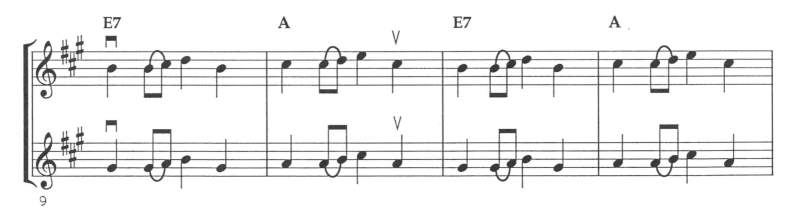

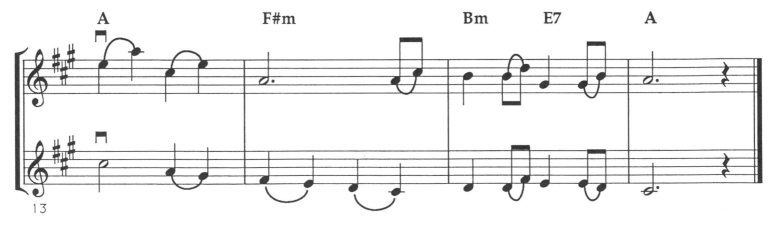

CHORD CHART

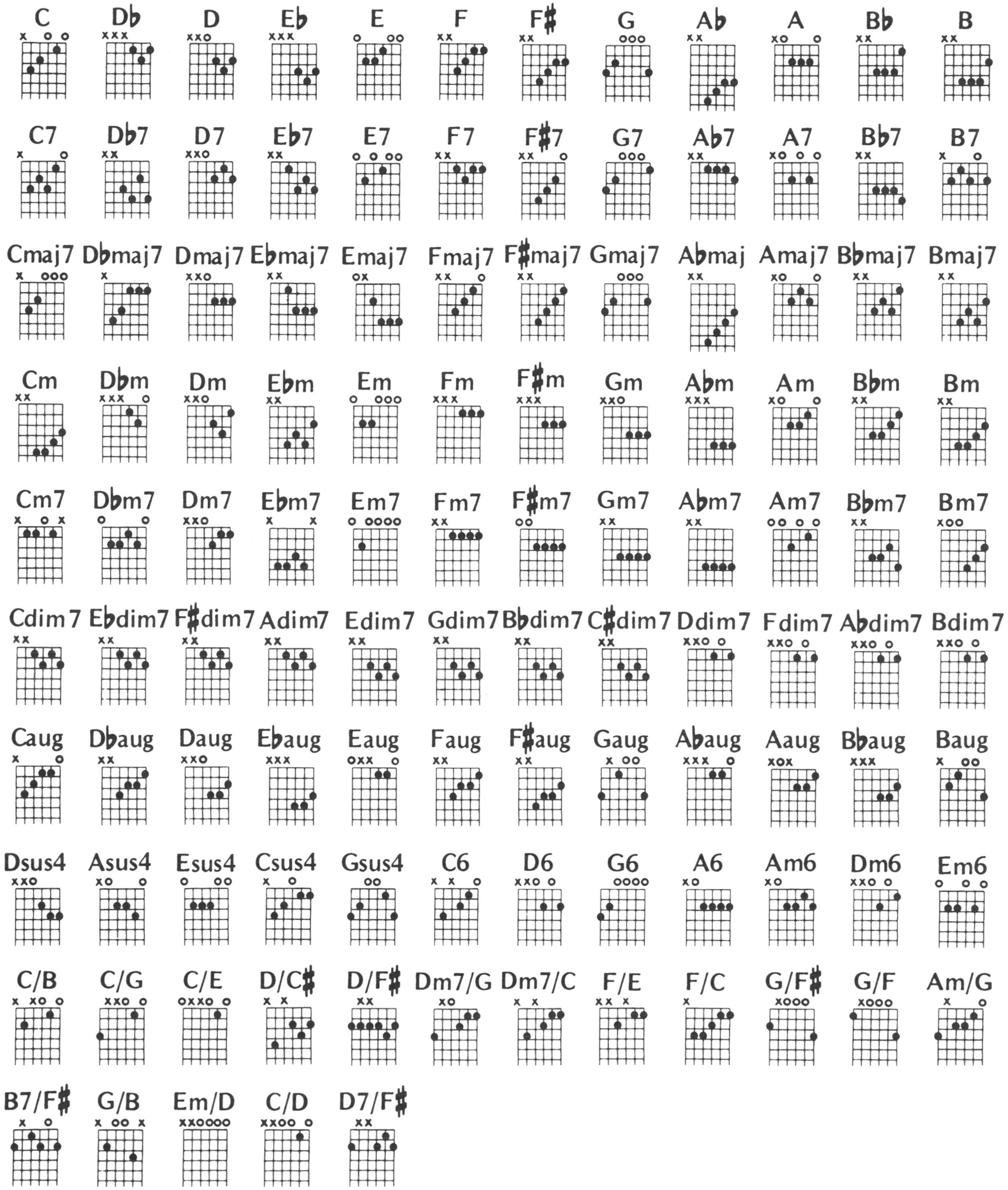
C D♭ D E♭ E F F♯ G A♭ A B♭ B
C7 D♭7 D7 E♭7 E7 F7 F♯7 G7 A♭7 A7 B♭7 B7
Cmaj7 D♭maj7 Dmaj7 E♭maj7 Emaj7 Fmaj7 F♯maj7 Gmaj7 A♭maj Amaj7 B♭maj7 Bmaj7
Cm D♭m Dm E♭m Em Fm F♯m Gm A♭m Am B♭m Bm
Cm7 D♭m7 Dm7 E♭m7 Em7 Fm7 F♯m7 Gm7 A♭m7 Am7 B♭m7 Bm7
Cdim7 E♭dim7 F♯dim7 Adim7 Edim7 Gdim7 B♭dim7 C♯dim7 Ddim7 Fdim7 A♭dim7 Bdim7
Caug D♭aug Daug E♭aug Eaug Faug F♯aug Gaug A♭aug Aaug B♭aug Baug
Dsus4 Asus4 Esus4 Csus4 Gsus4 C6 D6 G6 A6 Am6 Dm6 Em6
C/B C/G C/E D/C♯ D/F♯ Dm7/G Dm7/C F/E F/C G/F♯ G/F Am/G
B7/F♯ G/B Em/D C/D D7/F♯